They Say that I Am Two

Poems by
Marcos McPeek Villatoro

Arte Público Press
Houston, Texas
1997

This volume is made possible through grants from the
Cultural Arts Council of Houston/Harris County, the
National Endowment for the Arts (a federal agency)
and the Andrew W. Mellon Foundation.

Excerpts from "The Hollow Men" and "Ash Wednesday" in COLLECTED
POEMS 1909-1962 by T.S. Eliot, copyright 1936 by Harcourt Brace &
Company, copyright © 1964, 1963 by T.S. Eliot, reprinted by permission of
the publisher. Excerpts from "La United Fruit Company" and "Significa
sombras" by Pablo Neruda are reprinted with permission by La Fundación
Pablo Neruda, Santiago, Chile.

Recovering the past, creating the future

Arte Público Press
University of Houston
Houston, Texas 77204-2090

Cover design by Giovanni Mora
Book design by Debora Fisher

Villatoro, Marcos McPeek.
    They say that I am two / by Marcos McPeek Villatoro.
    p. cm.
    ISBN 1-55885-196-8 (alk. paper)
    I. Title.
PS3572. I386T48 1997
811'.54--dc20   96-39828
                                                     CIP

The paper used in this publication meets the requirements of the American National
Standard for Permanence of Paper for Printed Library Materials Z39.48-1984. ♾

They Say that
I Am Two

Poems by

Marcos McPeek Villatoro

To Ed "Mundo" Dunn

Also by the author:

−*A Fire in the Earth*
−*Walking to La Milpa - Living in Guatemala with Armies, Demons, Abrazos, and Death*

Table of Contents

Central America:
Walking the Sweet Waistline

La dulce cintura de América

Pablo Neruda

First Impressions

I thought that
war
was
black and
white
with
scratches on the screen.

Song for Menchez

Menchez, you speak to me
like laughter over leftover beans
and sweet crumbs floating in coffee.

We walked your streets of Jícaro,
asking for onions and eggs,
collecting *no hay*[1] at every market.
"Plenty of nothing," I joked.
Aguantar[2], you said,
prophesying with a smile
that you have been hungry before
and will know it again.

We slipped from the church
into the dry shards of April.
The old poet stumbled by,
two days shaveless
and rum boiling him dry.
Carlos Fonseca, la Tayacán,
Jesús y María nos atrazan.[3]
He rhymed it, again and again,
waiting for a response
from the sober public.

It was quiet those days,
like the bodies
they had dropped in the park,
leaving them for families
to gather after dark.
Putrid gifts from an enemy,
now neutral, once again family.
We poked around to see
if your son had come home.

We escaped to
your adobe stove,
drank your coffee
ate your pot of beans.
Once again, the rich man
eating the fruit of the poor.
This time a guest.
The taste of war, the monotony of
beans served on beans
with cold coffee
washing it down
day after day.
It was true life.

Have you met death?
Your daughters, dark as deep earth
and lithe as desire,
have they been burnt
by the fingers
of the violent ones?

I sit in my peaceful office
and speak to your spirit of early dawn,
obscure as leather,
rich as the smell of plowed soil.

Bertila

Today
Bertila turned
forty years and
sixteen pregnancies old.
High blood pressure
burst her open
in ten miscarriages.
She scrubs laundry
in the creek bed,
stretched a belly away
from the rock.

And over here
we'll find her man.
He rests weary, proud testicles
in a baggy hammock.

Six survivors
swim about her
and splash her drying clothes.
The rooted veins
wrap up her legs,
vined trees that plunge the water.

She beats those clothes.
Ask her of the pregnancy,
she offers all she knows:

Primero Dios.[1]

Her destiny
smiles toothlessly,
"Whatever my God wills."

Juxtaposition

Bertila birthed a *leñador*[1].
The woodchopper slashed at our life
with arms that searched for milk, no more.

While the street birthed heavier shades,
green midwives with raised machetes
stained the full moon with tossing blades.

Bertila brings him to the breast.
The nurses lay the street-birth on
a nearby bed to give it rest.

It stares, a Picasso-chopped face,
while doctors whisper facts outside,
"Soldiers," they say. "Silence this place."

The *leñador* finds his nipple
and asks nothing more of this night,
nothing of the clinic's ripple

of fright, or of ribboned faces.
Bertila holds her little man,
rushing him to other places.

Sex in El Petén, Guatemala

It was said that Ruth
slept at the feet of her man.

I touch the ankles and heels
of my woman,
and appreciate scripture.

The nerves untie themselves,
unwrap our bones
and slough off, dried out serpent skins
of vengeance.
The massage frees her body
from the soldiers who dance in
silent camouflage
outside our door.
Fingers grope
toward a kicking heart,
while a quetzal bird[1]
beats itself against the cage.
We all seek freedom.

We touch, and her fruit
bursts
with the wetness
of this jungle.
Our thighs
fill with a warm, living rain.
They drop a storm
and bathe us
in a spray
of forgetting.

The quetzal flies.

Ruth slept
at the feet of her man.
Thus she began
a horny liberation.

The Boy

We spent the day
collecting tears the kidnappers had
bequeathed a wife.
Piricón, a village sheltered by
flames that danced off mountains.
The dry season. Time to scorch the earth
and rouse a hopeful harvest.

The village gave us their treasures,
two tortillas
and a cup of coffee.

We set camp on sun-baked ground
that cooled under stars.
The mountains flickered
shadows on the war zone.
A boy from the village
dared to sit beside me.
He saw the fire in the hills
like gods that burst open
the heart of the earth.

Bob, my companion,
spoke in a weary cadence.
"They'd just die in Marin County."
Distant activist groups
fighting for the rights of trees
as we watched these hills burn clean.

We spoke in English.
The words whispered
mystery to the boy.
His eyes closed, an exhaustion
of witnessing too much in one day.

"*¿Estás cansado, vos?*" I asked, breaking his spell.
"*¿Querés acostarte?*"
"*Sí,*"[1] he smiled, taking my offer.

I pulled his thin weight to me,
rested his head upon my lap.
His hand drifted over my thigh
and dangled like a resting puppet
dashed upon stone.

The fire crawled down
and ate last year's corn stalks.
Its whisper crackled smoke that
rose with a north wind
to search for a kidnapped father.

I lay the boy beside me.
Bob and I rested on sleeping bags
and entertained ourselves with analyses
that only a gringo could think up.

The child drew near,
caressed the foreign Velcro
and held me in a boy's grip,
tight as this youth,
old as this war.

When the sun nudged us
he stumbled away,
his bare feet
wrapping sharp stones
like dry leather.

He returned.
Again, tortillas and coffee.
We ate and grumbled
over our filth and weariness.
The people bid us goodbye,
with a hope
that they could once again
be at our service.

I left them.

Tonight
I eat meat,
drink an imported beer,
and wear clothes, many clothes.
I weep
useless tears
as the boy bores out of my chest
and smiles upon the ache
of lavish impotency.

Final Hope

We walk
between marimbas and M-16s,
between ink pens and pyramids and
coffee and beans and borders.

Wind scatters them,
flings their story apart
in the spray of a dying vortex.
We come around,
collect the debris of the
disassembled body.
Now together, its dark mouth
filled with dust and blood cakes,
opens and screams.

The wail runs
like a rabid gunshot,
splitting open heaven
gorged with forgotten rain.

Dreamstate I

It was on the ocean front, where soldiers walked the streets, and women sold mangoes and oranges for fifteen córdobas each. We all waited. We had heard the news. Why did we look at one another and smile, periodically shaking hands?

I pushed the old man of my years up a long, muddy slide, that old worker, somehow wrenched out of me and put in this form. The elder muttered elegant, caustic prose as I pushed him toward the hill, unwritten phrases of future, hoped-for books and poems that had not come about because of the promise ahead of us, across the beach and ocean. I pushed him over the summit and sent him sliding down the hill, past soldiers and women with rosaries, all who muttered, "Poor bastard. He wanted to do so much."

I walked on the beach and whispered prayers of forgiveness, of readiness, hoping to be muttering the words, "My dear God," when the first one hit. And so it was. The blue light moaned over the ocean in waves of electric heat that steamed the salt water before it pelted me time and again. I moved along. I ran over the once-lovely sand as I felt my ankles shrivel and dissolve into the hot beach. I passed the hill and looked into the blue-glazed daylight. I saw the now-silent old man, deep gorges where his eyes had been, the muscles in his face dissolved, his melted jawbone with the singed goatee lopped off the skull and tumbling over his chest, hanging there by one elastic strand of ligament. Then the final light burst forth, and oh how the reefs in front of me curled in the heat of man's made ecstasy!

Permission

Two friends lay upon the wooden bed.
Joaquín stared at the ceiling while I changed his pants.
The black hole burned into his chest gave me the chance
To turn away from Michael's severed head.

Michael's doctor bragged about his art.
"The thread is thick and black, but you can barely see
The cut. It's my best work." I waited for his glee
To pass. We flung Joaquín on a cart,

Then turned to María who expired
With a tubercular breath I pushed from her chest
While lifting her. The lungs pressed empty, like the rest
Of these quarters. We had all grown tired.

The smell of day-old chicken ruined me.
I turned toward the living, a home, a meal, a drink.
They took me to a charred corn field where I could think
Of nothing, and smell the lone roast, free

Of olfactory reminders. Death
Chuckled at those who proclaim to have a mission.
Rotting chicken merely gives us the permission
to feel the passing of another's breath.

A Note to Carolyn Forché

after reading
The Country Between Us
for the twelfth time.

Your words
slipped over pages
like silk off an inner thigh.

I read them, and you
handled me with experience,
smiling as you watched me shake
with a young man's desire
to remember his forgotten country.

You walked in my people's blood,
held it in your hands
like a wounded lover's eucharist
and wept under its scream.
You dashed it upon paper
before it could die.

This may never reach you.
Each time I read you, I
hurry your words into my mouth
like an insecure lover.

Please forgive
the rantings of a stranger.

Lost in the Translation

I sit between a Chicago reporter
and a Nicaraguan woman,
holding both tongues
like the delicate chain between
truth and language.

> "Ask her what she does."

> > *I am a worker.*
> > *I am poor, and I*
> > *live to see my son.*

She pours coffee, laughs as
the gringo squints his moustache
above its sweetness.

> > *Poor thing. Cannot even*
> > *speak. Why is he here?*
> > *Out here?*

Here, between shrapnel and hunger,
hope and sovereignty spattered on tree limbs.

> > *My son fights for us all.*
> > *Stationed in San Juan.*
> > *I hope to see him soon.*
> > *A bunch of us mothers will*
> > *hitch rides through the mountain.*
> > *I will carry him*
> > *these candies you gave me.*

She holds the M & Ms, multicolored nuggets;
sweet promises of that other world.

> "I hear the enemy tries to kill
> mothers when they visit.
> Mines on the road, signs of their strength.
> What do you think?"

He sucks his filter, wiping first-world sweat
from his palid forehead.

She looks at me, coffee-eyes of innocence,
waiting for my interpretation.
I commit translator's treason.

> He says he prays that you may see your son.

She smiles, approving
the sympathetic gringo.

Truth and language whisper together
with the aromas of coffee and adobe
smacking against Polo Cologne.

— ⚜ —

On his cycle, he shifts gears toward the city.
He drops the filter to the ground,
but does not smash it.

"They'll pick it up later,"
he motions to the street boys,
"and stick them in their local brand."
He smiles, proud of the gift
dropped on the earth
like a spent seed of dependency.

I tell him, in the
language of the blunt ones,
"You know, you hit the nail upon the head."

Storyteller, gravedigger,
pounding the shovelled scoops of words and names
into your cemetery of a front page.

While Typing Reports

There are many to do.
These people are
made of paper.
I type them in,
process their blood and lost wives.
I program their rapes and cut throats
with the tapping quietude of computer keys.
Hundreds of reports float by my desk.
I have read them all. None have

Escaped. They have gathered
in my blocked cell.
Then a surprise visit, through
a concerti on the radio.
Bach, of all people, dances through dark halls
in my skull.
He skips about
like a child mathematician.
He decorates the darkness with first notes
alien to this third world,
rests in a melodic lilt at the metal door
and enters the key.

The door swings wide,
and Concerto Number Two rouses them up.
The machetes dance and slice.
Bullets make their rounds
to the F Major chord.
The screams of women
slip under the second movement's melody
and the grunting of a hot body.
The attackers slip away
into the nearby mountain,
leaving the violated flesh and earth
to be entertained
by a most harmonious crescendo.

In Teotucacinte

Along the Honduran Border

She was dark as new leather
and smiled like stars.

"You may stay with us."

She stood at her adobe door
with eyes encircling the day.
"It is quiet here," she said,
"though the enemy is near,"
pointing to the border
with wet lips.

Then she became another,
la revolucionaria,
and I listened as she told me
how her town was ready to fight and die
before the *yanqui*[1], before the contra.
"They killed my father and took my brother."
She spoke like a soldier
for that lonely moment.
Then, from a heart of
burdened necessity,
"You may stay with me."

The river rushed nearby,
the only relinquish
from that dusty season.
I walked away to work,
to find fresh death
apathetically organized
by those of my other blood.

She bathed in
shallow water that
poured from wells
where the enemy slept
by the dirtless grave
of her kidnapped brother.

Birthed from the river,
she combed back
her sole clothing of hair.
Her stare,
whipping with enraged beauty,
flung my blood
into thick liquid
and light foam.

"Te doy un hijo."[2]
You half-mixed gringo, come here to save my country.
I will give you an off-white baby
and when you leave, he will cry out
and he will fight for something true,
for half the blood that trickles in you.

Al mear

El joven que se envejecía de trago
fue a la trasera.
Vio las estrellas que se reían
en el cielo callado.
Pensaba, "Vivo, menos mal que
vivo".
Empapó la misma tierra
de ayer, y anteayer.
Respiró el aire limpio
e hizo una promesa:
respirar, a veces lento, a veces
jadeante,
pero que respirara con
pulmones que anhelaran llenarse
con la risa de las estrellas.

While Voiding

The young man who grew old with whiskey
went outside.
He watched the stars that laughed
in a silent sky.
He thought, "I'm alive. At least I'm
alive."
He soaked the same ground
from yesterday and the day before.
He breathed crisp air
and made himself a drunken promise:
To breathe, sometimes slowly,
other moments panting,
but to breathe with
lungs that longed to fill themselves
with the laughter of stars.

Los quejidos del escritor

Me levanto
a las cuatro y pico
para aprovechar un silencio desconocido.

Y gritan los animales.
Juegan los perros.
Una ola de gallos
hacen competencia
para ganar la madrugada.
Un gato se zafa por la grieta.
La vecina ha decidido
gozar un mariachi.
Ella cree que a todo el barrio
le gusta la música mexicana.

Aquí estamos,
todos los aullidos,
y la pluma que
sigue arrastrándose por la hoja
como si existiera una tranquilidad
como si venciese el silencio.

A Writer's Complaints

I rise
at four-thirty
to take advantage
of an unknown silence.

And the animals wail—
dogs play,
a wave of roosters
compete for the morning.
That cat squeezes through a fence's crack.
The neighbor has decided
to enjoy a mariachi band.
She believes that the whole *barrio*
likes Mexican music.

Here we are, with
everyone's yelps,
along with a pen that
keeps dragging itself over a sheet,
as if tranquility existed,
as if silence had won out.

Looking Back

I walked through a month
of burning buildings
and raped women.
Offbeat mortars
spurt through tree limbs.
Tanks danced in the dust
of a dying day.
Soldiers littered the park,
waiting for a battle cry
from the drunken sergeant.
The world's water steamed away
while running toward a cracked lip.
Life became as dry as these lines,
inspiration fruitful as a used cartridge.

Despedida de Poptun

Yo ando aquí
en los escombros de memorias,
en los estragos de experiencias
de una tierra enriquecida con jade y sangre,
una milpa amarilla, manchada con
la púrpura recién nacida,
sellada con las bendiciones
de cinco candelas prendidas
por una india anciana.

Mis últimos momentos como ambulante,
dando patadidas a las piedras ajenas,
como fotógrafo sin cámara, con la pluma
y la hoja empapadas de
lágrimas y carcajadas.

Vine, y me dijeron, "Que Dios le bendiga, Señor Gringo".
Me voy, dejando no sólo el terreno,
sino el regalo que tal vez me vaya a
rescatar el alma tan necia:
Las caras que se agachan hacia la tierra,
las manos que tortean el sol hasta que
se convierta en comida,
los ojos que se mojan en una despedida,
y las sonrisas que se atreven a decir,
"Ay, Marquitos, que te vaya bien, vos".

Goodbye, Poptun

I walk around
in the debris of memories.
Here, in a land enriched with jade and crimson,
a yellow corn field
stained with
recently birthed blood,
stamped with the blessings
of five burning candles
handled by an old Indian woman.

These are my final moments as an itinerant stone kicker,
acting like a photographer without a camera, with only a pen
and a sheet of paper soaking in tears
and laughter that splits a man's sides.

I came, and they said to me, "May God bless you, Mister Gringo."
I depart, leaving behind not just the land,
but a gift that may
ransom my stubborn and foolish soul:
the faces that stoop over, kissing the earth,
the hands that snatch at sunlight
and flip it into a stoveful of tortillas,
the eyes that wetten in a final goodbye,
and the smiles that dare to say,
"Oh, Marquitos, may it go well with you."

A Miguel Ángel Asturias

Escrito en las últimas páginas de Hombres de Maíz

Aquí estoy, don Miguel,
en un aeropuerto internacional,
lejos de las mujeres morenas
que andan con pies de cuero
y que tortean para que
el sol se caiga en el comal.

Aquí, donde no hay tierra,
sólo fronteras, sellos, pasaportes que
valen más que un cuerpo.
Los gringos se ponen alrededor
y los detesto, mientras hablan
de los colores de Guate, como
se compran baratos,
y de los inditos tan sencillos
y los movimientos de la civilización occidental.
("Páseme un cafecito por favor,
en una taza desechable".)
Los detesto, y ando a su lado.

Poco tiempo aquí, en la tierra suya,
conociendo a una parte de la vida
del hombre de maíz,
tocándonos, arriesgando una amistad aquí, allá,
dejando lágrimas y un hueco
de ecos retumbantes
en la jaula de mis costillas.

Tenga la bondad de permitirme

llevarlo usted a mi patria pasaporteada.
Para que sobreviva
los arranques de nervios
que han envuelto los huesos de la tierra
más allá de la ventanilla
de aviones, cemento y extranjeros.

Permítame pasaje a las obras suyas,
y aunque no lo conozca (sólo por cara
atrás de mis amigos poptunecos),
guíeme por las palabras y los párrafos,
por los colores, los hombres
agachados y con machete,
las mujeres torteando el sol,
para que sí, vuelva yo al país
picante del alma, Guatemala.

To Miguel Angel Asturias

Scratched on the back page of my copy of Hombres de Maíz

Here I am, don Miguel,
in an international airport
far from the dark women who
walk on leather feet
and who slap tortillas so that
the sun falls into the frying pan.

Here, where there is no earth,
only borders, stamps, passports
valued more than bodies.
The gringos stand around me,
and I detest them, as they speak
about Guatemalan colors, how cheap they are
to buy,
and those simple little Indians,
and the development of our western civilization.
("Pass me a coffee in a styrofoam cup, please.")
I hate them, while I walk with them.

I was in your land for a short while,
getting to know the corn man's life,
touching a few people,
risking friendships,
leaving a few tears and the hollow
vibration of echoes
under my ribs.

Please be so kind as to permit me
to carry you to my passported country.
Thus I may stunt the pain
of nerves ripped off
the bones of land that stands
beyond this plexiglass window, beyond
the jets, the cement,
the foreigners.

Allow me passage into your works.
Though I don't know you (except by sight-
behind the faces of chapín friends),
guide me through the words and
the paragraphs,
through the colors, the men
stooped over with machete in hand,
the women who make tortillas out of sunlight.
Thus, perhaps I can
return to your soul-pricking country,
Guatemala.

Transient Religious Moments

The supplication of a dead man's hand
Under the twinkle of a fading star.

T.S. Eliot

Cuando muera yo

Cuando muera yo,
ten la bondad de esconder en la caja
una copia de
Cien años de soledad.
Ponla en mi pecho.
Coloca un quinto de Johnnie Walker Red
bajo mi brazo.
Deja el rosario de mi abuelita
en un bolsillo del saco,
y una foto de mi güera querida
entre los dedos.

Así pues, estoy listo
a pavonearme, y cacarear del amor,
a tocar, finalmente, los abalorios negros,
a hojear el libro que se trata de
las fronteras olvidadas entre la
vida y la muerte.

Luego, por la tarde, yo
desenrosco la pacha,
y ofrezco un trago a los demás.
Mientras las copitas se tocan en brindis,
nos tronchamos de risas
sobre los muertos sonrientes
que siguen besando la tierra.

When I Die

When I die,
please sneak into the box
a copy of
One Hundred Years of Solitude.
Place it upon my chest.
Put a fifth of Johnnie Walker Red
snug in one arm.
You can slip my grandmother's rosary
in a coat pocket
and a photo of my lady
between my fingers.

Thus I'll be ready
to strut around, boasting about beauty;
to finger, finally, the little black beads;
and to thumb through the book on
the forgotten borders between
life and death.

Then, in the afternoons, I will
crack the seal,
and offer a round to anyone interested.
While the glasses click together,
we'll split our sides laughing
over the smiling dead
that continue kissing the earth.

Oda a los religiosos

Al pensar en
los que ven el tuétano humano
como la grasa en que
se ponen fritas sus prioridades,
me pongo un poquito nervioso.
Busco una salida
entre los ramos del bosque.

Yo me escabullo
bajo los golpes
de la catarata,

donde ya no me cuecen,
donde me encuentro desnudo
bajo un agua despiadada.
El chorro corre en
los huesos huecos y chamuscados.

Prenden el fuego.
Con collarín blanco
baten el tuétano ya
disuelto a puro aceite.
Me esperan al lado del agua,
mirándome el esqueleto con
lenguas que lamen los labios arrugados
de los santos.

Me baño.
Las yemas propias me buscan,
me erigen,
y aunque los huesos ya están vacíos,
menos el olor del tuétano
cocido a tocino,
lleno el agua con
la crema de mis carcajadas.

Ode to the Religious

When I think about those
who use human marrow as the
grease in which they
fry their priorities,
I get a little nervous.
I look for an opening
between forest branches.

I slip under
the beatings of
a waterfall,

where they no longer cook me.
Where I walk around naked
under merciless water.
The gush rushes through my
bones, burnt and hollow.

They light the fire.
With a white collar
they stir the marrow that has
melted into filmy oil.
They wait alongside the lake
looking at my skeleton with
tongues that lick the cracked lips
of saints.

I bathe.
My fingers raise the occasion.
My bones, empty of marrow
and smelling of bacon,
fill the water with
frothy laughter.

Isaac's View

The only mercy survived in the bondage.
His father tied the cords loosely,
using the softest hemp from the barn.
The rest twisted upward, a macabre prayer
to Caprice.
"God will provide, when we arrive,"
speaking with paternal truths.
The old man's eyes lowered
in avoidance or petition.
The hired hands waited behind as ordered,
leaving no witnesses.

A wind passed their way.
The boy heard nothing, save the
mob of babbled protests
screaming through his skull.
His father turned and dropped the knife.

As the old man took the ram
and drove the blade,
the child rubbed his wrists
and glanced at the holocaust's smoke
rising to clouds of purified jealousy.

Sacred Kills

Here, in the land of sacred kills,
The bodies fall in strewn array.
We snatch them up to wipe our ills,
The final duty of the day.

Polish the holy objects bright:
A lover's thigh; a burning cross;
Biblical tales that guide the sight
Of those who seek an unseen boss.

Redemption soaks these boney rags.
With deathly grace they've cleaned the spills
And learned the truth which never lags:
Here, in this land, the sacred kills.

Unsatisfied Enemy

I sit, as the strangers melt by,
excreting their lovesongs
with a douched, urinous smell.
I watch. The bitter moments

Smile at each other
while vomiting out of church doors.
Then there is my own moment.
He stares at me. Wrinkled eyes

Strap me in place.
Old suckling, his tongue bitter and cracked.
I am, momentarily, hardened and packed
before the singe begins.

Writhing in the heat, wrinkled, short, withdrawn,
I dissolve under his pooled breath.
My sole defense, a wish:
If only you were dead,
back in your hellish womb.

Counseling

For some of us who
gather in bleeding circles,
there is no word more painful
than "brother,"
no phrase more enraging
than "God the Father,"
no concept less empty
than "motherhood."

They sing the motto of our days:
"To focus on the family
will heal the wounds of errant ways."

I agree.
Focus on the family.
Aim carefully
and shoot to kill.

Dreamstate II

I pass by a cement university, buildings, little grass, much concrete and bricks. Individuals pass by, going to classes, looking without seeing. They don't even speak to colleagues. They walk like they were already dead.

A professor walks up to me, smiling. "Are you ready for the debate?" she asks me. I tell her yes. She takes me to a room.

I attend the debate. I listen, I say a few little comments. The others are intellectuals, you can tell by the way they masturbate their skulls in unison. The debate has no life, just pedantic dialogues. I remain seated, feeling an ember in my chest, but I don't want to share it with anybody here.

Outside the bombs begin. The whole world burns. The people continue walking. Some are completely dead. Flesh falls from their bones. Their skin has turned grey. But they keep walking, by God, paying no attention to the bombs that continue exploding behind. I pass by the YMCA and see the same thing: cadavers chatting with one another, bench pressing the weights while their veins and viscera push through rotted skin.

I have not escaped the radiation. My body dies, but like the rest, it continues to function. I leave, crying tears of acid that burn my cheeks. I try to escape the cement of this reality.

Over there, in the turn of the road, stand trees, a forest that I don't know but one that looks similar to other forests of my life. I draw near it, and while I leave the concrete and the dead I see the green of the wild. A wolf stands there. I don't know how, but I know him. He's beautiful, healthy, the colors of silver and brown. The radiation has not affected his muscles. The poison hasn't been able to touch the hot blood that runs through his veins, one that pumps through the tongue that hangs between his teeth. Pure beauty. He stares at me and waits. I walk nearer. As sick as I am, I'm embarrassed to put myself before such a wondrous animal.

Standing before the wolf, I see that the skin of my arms has turned gray, like the others. I tremble. My tears filled with toxic trash fall to the earth. The wolf stares at me. Now I only see the wolf's face, his brilliant, obscure eyes, the thick hair, the wet nose that reflects the stars.

From the middle of my heart a voice screams, perhaps the last piece of my being known as Marcos. The supplication falls over cracked lips, "Please."

The wolf responds. His mouth opens. His brilliant teeth, with the baptism of his saliva, jump to me. I see the face of the wolf disappear underneath my chin. I feel the teeth plunge into the skin of my rotted neck, the coat around his mouth now underneath my cheeks. His jaw closes with seven hundred pounds of pressure, crushing my esophagus, arteries, the vertebrae inside my throat. Thank you. Thank you.

A Christology

He now wished he took no stock
in garden promises,
in leaving it all up to someone
who never told everything.
He looked up, but could not find a father;
he dropped his head, saw a weeping mother.
A thorn touched his skull, bursting
a full wineskin of memories.

"An order came in for the murderer
who spoke of zealot ideas, but spoke too loud,
and killed a man while in a drunken stupor.
They need a cross, boy. Fetch me the timber."
The carpenter's son ran off in glee
since his father asked him for help.
But his tender hands could not hold the beams
and splinters shoved into his palms.
The woodmaster laughed. His son was still too young
to do a man's job.

She cried. She thought she felt his kick
inside her empty womb.
Who would think it should end this way?
He was born in wood, that place, so uncomfortable.
Carpentry never brought in a living
and his preaching left her all the poorer.
Now where are his friends? Worthless cowards.
And where are you while you die?
The times he came in late, the times she worried
about him working in the carpenter shop
or hanging around kids she did not know
or scolding him for not picking up his clothes.

The countless times he fell in love,
"He always spread his heart too thin,
saying 'I love you' in too easy fashion."
She moaned at her own past tense and
leapt up to touch his face that
cried blood over his beard.
She screamed. Over thirty years of labor
to prepare for one death.

Rain fell. Someone was weeping.
I cannot say who. Analogies are never enough
to explain purpose.
I did not know him from so long ago,
though he peacefully hangs upon my wall.
Perhaps if he writhed and twisted,
I could grasp the meaning of his end
and comprehend the necessary birth.
But should I be glad of another's death?

Momentary Eschatology

Forgive me for my reference to God.
I know such thoughts are better left conceived
By those who wrap their problems in a shroud
And toss the sack toward a promised land
Teeming with sweet white folks and nice black gents
Who made their peace so ahistorically.
Forgive me. God's not in Bennetton ads.
The colors have united. That's our fix.
There is no need for tricks of faith or leaps.
So please overlook my wispy reference
To the road that I ran upon today,
The one I sprint on every day. The years
On this mountain have kept the mountain still.
The yelping dogs now know me all too well.
Their barks are meant to be mere protocol.
I do not know what happened. When I stopped
I was alone. A wind played with my breath.
You know the scene: blue sky, blue lake, thick trees.
I will not waste the poetry on these.
The dogs on porchsteps may have thought me stopped
By the calling of my name, such as they
Whose ears leap to catch familiar voices
In a whispered wind. I was not happy.
Happiness is for those who have let go.
Then something did let go: Time swung about
And snatched at my neck like a tetherball
Whose rope is far too long. Please indulge me.
I slip into the thick folds of the shroud.

I returned home. In later, measured days
The letter arrived. Cain shoved his fingers
Into the ground and snatched at Abel's wrist.
The rape happened long ago. No shaking
Could clean that dust off. Let's not be naive.
Faith taught me leaps. Life taught me, "Tie your shoes."
Yet Cain acted. It was enough to scrape
The brittle calcium upon my bones.
I almost heard it shatter on the floor
Had not the world caught it on a cushion
Of perfect sound-bites and virtual love.
So I ask a final time, forgive me,
Real world of Bennetton, for all my sins
Of momentary leaps, stripped of reason.
For when I ran again, the hillock stood
Waiting for my editorials on
Tetherball concepts of time that snap chronology.
The petition of forgiveness lay before my shoes
Twenty-eight years after violations,
When its arrival cracked the calcium
And my bones flew through a heated run
And I muttered illogical questions
To the mountain, "Did you know? Did you always know?"

They Say...

"Ay, que lo que yo soy siga existiendo
y cesando de existir".

Pablo Neruda

"HURRY UP PLEASE ITS TIME"

T.S. Eliot

Preliminaries

With fountain pen in hand, I pump
A revolution from my skull.

Aching beliefs pile in a dump.
Organizers carry their dull

Slogans to protest my action.
They're as bad as the religious.

Yet I do not mourn my faction.
They'll carry on in their prestigious

Enthusiasm for a people's cause,
Though lacking in the necessary pause.

While You Were Gone
(Song to the Compulsive Orderly)

To Michelle

I see you everywhere.
In sacred plastic bags,
a pile of radical rags,
a list, telling of another list
that straightens out life in a row
of things to do.
I grow listless, and wait
for your return when
you will show love in order
and desire in a choreographed day.

Miscarriage

To Michelle

As the laurel withers over
to kiss the earth goodbye,
somewhere
rain falls,
weeping upon a land that
pulses with cries of thanksgiving.

The stem snaps upon itself.
Raindrops are enough to
bring it to its roots,
as if to beg for mercy.

It is the sadness of
sensitive soil that
digs the grave,
the humble wail of
wind that warns us, do not
forget, do not forget.

It is the sun
over your wounded body that
heals the threadroots of endeavor,
drying the blood
of your silent ordeal.

Then the night that wearies you,
splashing darkness upon your skin,
spattered blessings of exhaustion.

⋯⋯ ▰◆▰ ⋯⋯

The healing never shall begin
nor end. Fuck this. We are not flowers.
We are not flowers.

History

To Vicki A.

As a man I am
born in the lackness of men.

A spontaneous jest,
a moment of thoughtless
bonding with a colleague
twists into history,
impales a memory, and
cleaves the old wound open.

"A year ago he took me from behind."

We choke and embrace in
double apologies,
knowing of our present tense
flooded with the imperfect past.

I am man, attacker,
memorable rapist of memory.
I never could take back the night.
I rend the day, and cover a new friend
with old darkness.

I join the attacker.
It was his story, given unto me.

Ode to an Avocado

I eat an avocado.
They valued it at ninety eight cents.
In old days and mother countries
that meant five thousand *córdobas*.
Enough to buy six beers
or a night at a stale inn
with one large bucket of water
for two sweaty lovers.

This little green traveler
has seen too much.
Tossed by calloused hands, it
could have dropped into the sea, like
so many dead Indians from the dock.

If it were priced at twenty cents,
old *compañeros* would laugh at me,
pricing an avocado like a
smile, or a kiss stolen deeply
within the open branches
of an orchard.

At ninety eight, they turn their eyes from me,
looking away from an ignorant *patrón*
who holds the fruit of their labor
in his soft hand.

Este día de nuestra vida

Hoy en la mañana doña Juanita
chineaba la cabeza de
su hijo Juan Ramón,
ya abierta por el balazo
que él se regaló.

Acostado en la caja,
las lágrimas de formaldehido
cruzaron su mejilla
y los padres gritaron al dueño
de la funeraria
de la resurrección de su hijo mayor.

Lo enterramos
en el calor humeante de la boca de junio.
Todos los dolientes eran de Guanajuato.
Ellos limpiaban sus caras
con dedos manchados de la tierra de tomate,
y arrancaron a la madre
de los manillares de la tumba.

En la tarde
visitamos al nuevo chicano
que nació en un hospital de Birmingham.
Lo llamaron Jesse,
su propia traducción de Jesús,
también un nombre
que promete ser aceptado
por un mundo gringo.
Jesse dormía, y su respiración
se zafaba como los zumbidos

de abejas perezosas.

⸻

En la noche
nos huimos a un comedor mexicano
donde los meseros
convirtieron un rincón de Birmingham
en un mundito latino.
Noche de mariachi,
y el jefe gordo, vestido de negro
con rayas de plata que
caía como catarata
en su pantalón,
coqueteaba con la gringa borracha
hasta que ésta se prorrumpió
en un orgasmo de carcajadas.

Luego el gordo
cantó un toque para Paty,
"Yo Soy de San Luis Potosí".
Mi amiga se inclinaba en la mesa,
con el tenedor y las muletas a un lado.
Sus recuerdos volaban
como águila suelta
por las calles de
su barrio.
El gordo nos ganó,
y luego anunció
un Tequila Break.

⸻

Al volver a casa,
no nos dijimos nada,
sabiendo que este día de nuestra vida
era pregonero de todo.

This Day in Our Life

This morning doña Juanita
rocked the head of her
son Juan Ramón,
opened by a bullet that
he gifted himself.

Lying in the box,
he cried tears of
formaldehyde
over his cool cheeks.
His parents screamed to
the funeral director,
sharing the good news of
their oldest son's resurrection.

We buried him
in the humidity of June's closed mouth.
All the mourners were from Guanajuato.
They wiped their faces
with fingers stained from tomato fields,
then tore the mother away
from the tomb's railing.

In the afternoon
we visited the new chicano
born in a Birmingham hospital.
They named him Jesse,
their own translation of Jesús,
also a name that
promised to be accepted
into a gringo world.
Jesse slept, and his breaths

slipped away like the buzz
of lazy bees.

That night we
fled to a Mexican restaurant
where the waiters
turned a corner of Birmingham
into a tiny Latino world.
Mariachi night.
The fat leader, dressed in black
with silver lines cascading down
his pants,
flirted with a drunk gringa
until she burst open
in an orgasm of laughter.

Then the fat mariachi
sang a song to Paty,
"I am from San Luis Potosí."
My friend rested upon the table
with her fork and her crutches to one side.
Memories flew like a freed eagle
over the streets of her barrio.
The band's leader won us over,
then shouted for *un Tequila Break.*

When we returned home
we spoke of nothing,
knowing that this day in our life
had made enough statements.

Cuando nos tumbó la pata[1]

Cuando nos tumbó la pata,
vi las noticias
de la tele
y Paty se escondió
en el armario.

Pura casualidad que mi amiga
nos visitaba durante el golpe de estado,
cuando la migra se bajó de los helicópteros
y corrió como serpiente loca
exprimiendo aun las calles del campo.

En las noticias, al cumplir bien
sus deberes
sin necesidad de inteligencia,
se habló del rescate de
500 empleos robados
por hombres mexicanos.

No me moví mientras
las familias se huían
a los bosques
y un amigo fue detenido
para que la migra confiscara su troca
llena de cobijas y almohadas.

Los niños, pues, se acurrucaban
entre los pechos de una mamá
que vigilaba los ruidos
nocturnos de la montaña.

Me quedé impotente
mientras el baile de un pecado legal
danzaba afuera,
riéndose, con un mal ojo tirado por la ventana
antes de tocar a la puerta.

Abrí el ropero.
Allí se acostaba la bella amiga ilegal,
bajo las muletas,
dos barrotes que
protegían los latidos
de un corazón enjaulado.

***

Tumbados, pero no tullidos.
Me dicen que
los primos deportados desayunaron
hoy en Monterrey
y cenaron de nuevo en Houston.

Y mañana almorzarán
en un truck stop de Birmingham

mientras las montañas aquí, pues,
se madrugaron en el olor
ocultado de tortilla
y el vapor de frijol hervido.

When the Paw Brought Us Down[1]

When the paw brought us down
I watched the news
and Paty hid away in a closet.

Bad timing that my friend
paid a visit during the state of siege,
when *La Migra* dropped from helicopters
and ran like a crazed serpent, squeezing
life out of the deepest country backroads.

The news, never allowing intelligence
to stand in the way of doing their work,
spoke of the recovery of
five hundred jobs stolen by Mexicans.

I made no moves, while
families fled into the woods
and a friend was detained
while *La Migra* confiscated his truck
filled with pillows and blankets.

The children nestled into breasts
of mothers who kept vigil over
the nocturnal noises
running through the mountain.

I stood, impotent
while the dance of a legal sin
frolicked right outside
laughing as he flicked the evil eye
through my window
before knocking on the door.

I opened the closet.
Our lovely illegal friend
lay under her crutches,
two bars that defended
the dolorous throb of
a caged heart.

Brought down, perhaps, but not maimed.
They tell me that deported cousins
ate breakfast in Monterrey
and supped in Houston.

Tomorrow they'll have lunch
in a Birmingham truck stop.

The mountains here?
They awoke to the hidden odor of tortillas
and the rising steam of boiled beans.

Dreamstate III

It was time to help a friend, and damned if I even know who the friend was.

He was having problems with a gang. I planned to stay with him for the night. We ended up in a small house. He hid in the ceiling, while I waited below.

Nothing happened. I said, "I better head home." He was nervous still, so I waited around a little longer. We heard noises. Someone was outside the house. Both he and I had small pistols. We drew them. I ran deeper in the house.

The doors burst open and men rushed in. I could not see their faces. In moonlight I could make out figures. They scrambled into corners.

I held my gun up. Light burst upon us like sudden day. I could see people outside through a large picture window. They approached the house, then drew back a step.

Before the night's darkness had dissipated, I drew a bead on one of the men and shot him. I wounded him in the arm. The hammer of my gun jammed, which was strange. It was a nine millimeter parabellum; its hammer should never jam.

Then came the morning sunlight and the people outside. The men who had burst in had captured my friend and had knocked me down to the floor. I heard one voice, "That's it, friend, you played the game too far." He placed his large pistol to me, the barrel's hole two inches from my forehead, and pulled.

I can now still hear the report, the sudden 'pop' that cracked through just above my left eye, and I can feel my skull as it rattles like a metal pole in a hollow log. Then my head goes limp, and the man stands over me, waiting for me to die. I look down and see my chest still moving up and down, and I think, "If he would only go away, I'll hold my breath so he'll think I'm dead. He'll go away. Then I'll get up."

I suppose he walks away. I'm not sure. I'm not in the

house anymore. I'm on a small hill, and there are wisps of fast-moving clouds passing by. This place is familiar. There are no buildings, only these grassy knolls, with a road to my right, going up the hill. This is my neighborhood in Tennessee, only, these clouds flying by, and the careful moan of a wind is all I see and hear. I feel no pain. In a far distance, I hear land being beaten by the sea.

I stand up, saying in a mumble, "Well, it was burdensome at times."

I am light, not as light as these clouds, but getting that way. I flow up the hill, almost following the road, and through the breaking clouds I see houses, that one of the Vaughn family, Glenn Martin's home, and below his, the Snodgrasses, and Colliers'. A twelve-year-old girl runs through the Vaughn's back yard. I yell to her, "Goodbye, Suzie. I always had a crush on you. I loved you like a boy only could, knowing you would be a gorgeous woman." Susan does not hear me. She plays on as I get lighter, and I flow past her. I move beyond the Snodgrasses, and over the road. I move over that front yard, the largest on the block, the one Dad hated to mow. There is the weeping willow, over the creek. There is the driveway, and it is asphalted. This is not the past at all; this is the world's present. There is the newly con-structed screened-in patio, now passing my left, and there before me is Michelle. She is dressed in a black skirt, one I have not seen before, and a white, fluffy blouse. She does not hold the kids, for they are playing near the rosebush box. My son José David is asleep somewhere. My two girls play. My mother is in the kitchen, preparing food, though she is as well dressed as my wife. Michelle's head is down slightly in that silence which I know. Her hands are barely in her skirt pockets, and she tosses a weary glance to secure the girls' safety.

I call out to Michelle, telling her I'm all right. It is not enough, and for the first time since rising from the grass on the other side of the neighborhood, I feel sadness. I reach out to touch both sides of her face as I speak. In the kitchen Mom turns and looks out. She smiles, as it seems so clear to her. "Look, Michelle, there's Marcos. He's saying goodbye." She sees, perhaps because of age, wisdom, perhaps for being a Latina. I'm not sure. She calls out to Dad, who's in back of the house. He mutters, "Oh yeah?"

My hands cannot touch Michelle's cheeks, nor her watery eyes. Nor can my words comfort her, especially as I grow lighter. I swerve around her like a ball flying itself from a centerpiece, held to it by a thread that finally snaps. Before it breaks I kiss her. My lips feel nothing, nor do hers.

"I love you, Michelle, please, be happy." But my own words fail me as I realize I will never feel her again, and as I turn and see the playing girls, all that I leave behind, and as the string snaps, and I fling away from my beloved wife toward the forest beside my parents' house, I scream no, no I can't. I flicker like the flame of a candle flung over someone else's cliff. I hear wind, and in the narrowing distance, the sea.

Ode to D

The D chord
plays like an innocent virgin
who's not ashamed to pray or yelp
Allelujah! to a grimacing stranger.

D ends an easy round of Rocky Top
only to begin a chorus of De Colores.

But lift your middle finger and you'll find
the lies that the virgin tucked away
long ago, some years back when
a handsome stranger made promises
as he lowered his head
between the spread of her strings.

D will then cry, and
sing a song of nostalgia.
She will undress, and
plea for another chord to catch her
before plummeting off the guitar neck.

I play her while lying on my bed.
The sun sets on a present day
of children running through the house,
tripping the air with laughter.
They bring tension to its knees.

She floats over me.
I tease her with a touch of G
only to lift up my finger
and listen to her weep.

She makes promises
that cannot be broken.
At least, not by herself.

Dicen que soy dos

Dicen que soy dos.
La sangre es un líquido que corre
entre hueso e hígado,
por los pasillos de los pulmones y los muslos oscuros.

La sangre conoce sólo un cuerpo.

La Ciudad del Hombre, como caprichona,
me ha obsequiado dos etiquetas:
blanca y morena.
Dicen que la blanca es la óptima.
Nadie me explica por qué,
como si hubiera una verdad
que se cayó de una nube
donde se sienta Mister Dios que escupe bendiciones
a los güeros
y maldiciones
a los demás.

La sangre conoce sólo un cuerpo.

He visto cuerpos abiertos,
la obra del navajazo, el arte del M-16.
Ayer chineaba la barriguita
de un cipote listo para dar a luz
un millón de lombrices.

La púrpura
sale a chorros,
y azota las calles
buscando raíces.

La sangre conoce sólo un cuerpo.
La sangre que conoce la tierra,
que se ha desparramado por las
piedras y las montañas, sin permiso,
es la sangre preferida.

They Say that I Am Two

They say that I am two.
Blood is a liquid that passes by chance
between bones and livers,
through passageways of lungs and inner thighs.

Blood knows only one body.

The City of Man, capricious as it is,
gave me two labels:
white and dark.
They've proven that white is more desirable.
No one tells me why, as if it were a truth
that fell from a cloud
where Mr. God sits, spitting blessings
upon gringos
and curses on the rest.

Blood knows only one body.

I have seen open bodies.
The work of the jagged edged blade,
the art of the M-16.
Yesterday I rocked to sleep
the inflated stomach of
a boy who gave birth
to a million worms.

The crimson gushes forth.
It whips the streets
in search of roots.

Blood knows only one body.
Blood flicked upon the sun-baked stones and
spattered upon adobe walls
must be the blood of preference.

Fathers on the Water's Edge

To Ralph

Yesterday I walked
on the Mississippi banks.
I listened to the hiss
of a July day.
Smelled fish carcasses
hidden behind thick weeds.
Walked on paths that were
smooth with the feet of
a thousand black men
baiting hooks for their sons.

I know these smells.
I know the
June bugs that
screech through
a Southern heat.

I have no fear of snakes
nor am I bothered by mosquitoes.
Even the humidity feels good,
slapping me awake
from my air-conditioned slumber.
What strikes fear in
the heart of city folk
welcomes me like
laughter from porch swings.
I am, after all, a Southerner.

My father
baited my hook
and pinched the arrow's clip
so as to fit it snug
onto the chord
of the arched bow.
I learned patience.

No petty anger in these woods,
nor on the river's edge.
No cursing over a lost bolt,
no slurred words thick with whiskey.
No tainted memory of shame,
though the siblings still play games
taught by naked relatives
who hide in shadows.

Here, I escape.
In the woods
and on the riverbanks
Dad blessed his son with
squirrel blood
and cool water from Big Creek.

We squatted in the woods
and measured our own time,
neither slow nor fast.
We held the bows like anxious warriors.
We tossed ten-pound test lines
into those silent creeks,
spat tobacco on the shore,
drank sodas, and waited
for the floater to bob.

Dad taught me silence in the forest.
Each time he skinned a rabbit
and gutted a blue gill
I learned how life ends quickly,
without a scream.

—————

Animal blood is a cleanser.
It sprays right through you, and
drives the nude ancestors away,
as if they were afraid
of being skinned themselves.

He taught me survival techniques
against our own.

Oda a Pablo Neruda

Ando en el estruendo del día,
el teléfono, la radio,
la televisión que me da
la vida de plástico, la muerte de cartón,
respiración de la luz brillante
que yo apago, por fin.

Y echo la culpa a
otros ruidos:
mi hija, sus gritos
que sólo son mensajes,
espejos de los adultos mocosos:
El que está en la cárcel,
otro que me exige que
organice la protesta,
los que dominan el dinero,
ellos que sirven a Cristo hasta el carajo.
Todos me buscan, y yo me huyo,
y apenas distingo.

Sería mejor, pues,
si no hubiera enfrentado a la policía
aquella tarde, en una universidad
de la juventud,
pensando apenas en una gente negra
del otro lado del Atlántico.
Si hubiera seguido caminando,
buscando a mi profesor, la biblioteca,
poniendo dos libros gruesos a
los lados de la cabeza,
mirando adelante, puro caballo.

¿Seré yo poeta? ¿Escritor,
autor de libros y de mentiras,
fumando puros, tomando cognac,
abriendo los muslos
de las mujeres que
anhelaran llenar la vaciedad de
un compromiso transeunte y literario?

O mejor, tal vez, como don Pablo,
pidiendo silencio de vez en cuando,
un momento calladito dentro
del estrépito de una lucha.
Buscando cinco raíces escogidas,
las hojas, el aguacero,
la sandía dentro del calor,
el amor que no tiene fin,
el verano redondo de mi mujer,
sus muslos blancos,
la rosa única de su pubis.

Así son mis anhelos, pues.
Casi nada, siempre todo.

Con tal que haya lápiz
que construya los momentos,
la hoja que se empape
del beso perfecto,
la oración que capte
la cachondez
de una respiración jadeante.

Ode to Pablo Neruda

I walk in today's chaos,
the telephone, the radio,
the television that gives me
plastic life, cardboard death,
the breath of a brilliant light
that I flip off.

I blame the other noises:
my daughter, her cries
that are merely messages,
mirrors of the adult brats:
He who is in jail;
the other one who demands
I organize the protest march;
those over there who hold the money;
and that final group, who serves Christ all the way to Hell.
They all look for me, and I flee,
distinguishing nothing.

It would be better
if I had not confronted the police
that afternoon, in that university
of youth,
when I barely thought about black folk
who lived on the other side of the Atlantic.
If I had only kept walking,
Seeking out my professor, the library,
putting the thick books on both sides of
my head, staring forward like a horse.

Would I have become a poet? A writer,
author of books and other lies,
smoking Havanas and drinking cognac,
opening the inner thighs
of women who
long to fill their emptiness with
a literary, transient promise?

Or better, perhaps, as don Pablo says,
to ask for silence from time to time,
a tiny quiet moment
inside the uproar of a fight.
Looking for five selected roots:
the pages, the rain,
a watermelon found under the sun,
an unending love,
the round summer of my woman,
her white thighs,
the one rose of her pubis.

Well, that's all I want.
Almost nothing, always everything.

As long as a pen is in reach
so as to construct the moments;
a sheet of paper soaked
with the perfect kiss;
the phrase that captures
some of the hot breath.

After These Moments

Still, he wondered
whether or not
it was necessary
to move the
wind
so as to
validate
his existence.

Notes on the Poems

Song for Menchez: [1]no hay = there is none;
[2]Aguantar = be patient; [3]Carlos Fonseca, la Tayacán, Jesús y María
nos atrasan. = "Carlos Fonseca, the Phoenix of hope, Jesus and
Mary set us back."

Bertila: [1]Primero Dios. = God first.

Juxtaposition: [1]leñador = woodcutter

Sex in El Petén, Guatemala: [1]The quetzal bird of Guatemala,
known for the long, green feathers of its tail, is a symbol of libera-
tion. After only a few hours in a cage, the quetzal dies.

The Boy: [1]"¿Estás cansado, vos?" = "Are you tired?"; "¿Querés
acostarte?" = "Do you want to sleep?"; "Sí," = "Yes,"

In Teotucacinte: [1]yanqui = Yankee; [2]"Te doy un hijo." = "I'll give
you a child."

Cuando nos tumbó: [1]En junio de 1995 El Servicio de Inmigración
y Naturalización hizo su proyecto llamado "Operation South
Paw". PAW significaba, en inglés, "Proteger trabajadores esta-
dounidenses". La Migra expulsó del sur de Los Estado Unidos a
miles de mexicanos sin documentos. Una tercera parte de nuestra
comunidad de Alabama desapareció en una noche, dejando a
niños esperando con las niñeras a madres que nunca llegaron.

When the Paw Brought Us Down: [1]In June of 1995, the United
States Immigration and Naturalization Service began "Operation
South Paw." PAW stood for "Protect American Workers." The
INS carried away thousands of undocumented Mexican workers
from the southeast. One third of the community in our area of
Alabama disappeared overnight, with children waiting in daycares
for mothers who never arrived to pick them up.